PUPPY LOVE

TABLE OF

CONTENTS

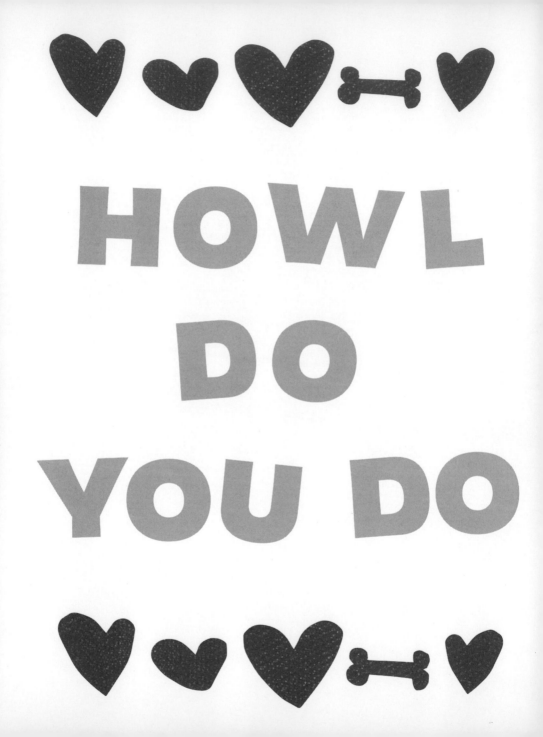

Maybe you're bringing home a new puppy for the first time. Maybe you've had your four-legged friend for years. Whatever your story may be, it's probably safe to assume that life is so much sweeter (and sillier) with your adorable pup in your home.

REMEMBER THAT TIME YOUR DOG...

- ♥ Cuddled up to you the first time?
- ♥ Ate that slice of pizza off your plate?
- ♥ Peed on the carpet before guests arrived?
- ♥ Made up for it by giving you the cutest look ever?

Consider this journal your spot to document all of your dog's most adorable, crazy, mischievous moments. From first birthdays and howlidays to begging habits and great escapes, this book is your place to record every pawsitive day in your life together.

before the first
BARK

*what was life even
like before you?*

I knew I wanted a dog when...

....

....

....

....

Who I had to convince...

....

....

....

....

How I started looking...

....

....

....

....

How long I had to wait...

....

....

....

....

My experience with dogs before you...

....

....

....

....

I was most excited about...

....

....

....

....

I was most nervous about...

....

....

....

....

How I picked you...

....

....

....

....

our first
pic together

LOVE AT first LICK

the day we met

Where I got you...

◯ ....

How it went down...

....

....

....

....

....

....

....

....

....

....

....

....

....

....

....

How prepared (or unprepared) I was to bring you home...

....

....

....

....

....

(check one below)

⬤ prepared

⬤ unprepared

My first thoughts about you...

....

....

....

....

....

....

....

....

Your first thoughts about me...

....

....

....

....

....

....

....

....

....

Other people who tagged along...

add a picture or list them out

↙

Your name when we first met...

....

pup-a-razzi
photo here

*pup-a-razzi
photo here*

BEST ❀DOG❀ EVER

The story behind your name...

....

....

....

....

....

....

....

All of your nicknames...

....

....

....

....

....

....

Words I use to describe you...

....

....

....

....

....

....

What was happening in the world when I got you...

....

....

....

....

YOUR BIRTH

♥ date of birth ....

♥ gotcha day ....

♥ full name ....

♥ gender ....

♥ height ....

♥ weight ....

♥ breed ....

♥ fur color(s) ....

♥ eye color(s) ....

CERTIFICATE

your zodiac sign

your birthstone

Garnet   Amethyst   Aquamarine   Diamond   Emerald   Alexandrite

Ruby   Peridot   Sapphire   Pink Tourmaline   Topaz   Blue Topaz

song topping the charts when i got you

....

BONE

SWEET

BONE

our first days together

The first home you lived in with us was...

draw your house here

Address ....
....

Your first car ride home...

draw your car here

The Story ....
....
....
....
....
....
....
....

Your first bed...

draw your pup's bed here

Your first night sleeping in our home...

....

....

....

....

....

Date..

Your first collar...

color your pup's collar here

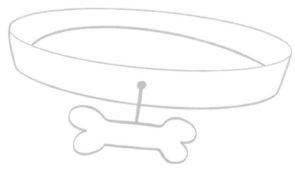

22

Meeting the family for the first time...

The Story..

....

....

....

....

....

....

Date...

The first time you cuddled up to me...

....

....

....

Your first toys...

....

....

....

Your first meal...

....

Your first trip to the vet...

....

....

....

....

....

Date..

Where we went on your first walk...

....

Things you loved on your first walk...

....

....

....

....

Things you didn't love on your first walk...

....

....

....

....

Your first neighborhood dog friend...

Name ....

How you met ....

....

....

....

Your first neighborhood human friend...

Name ....

How you met ....

....

....

....

The first things you barked or howled at...

....

....

How much I spent on my first shopping trip for you...

a lot   *more than i
should have*   *i am
embarassed*

BARKING UP
the family tree

your human and four-legged family

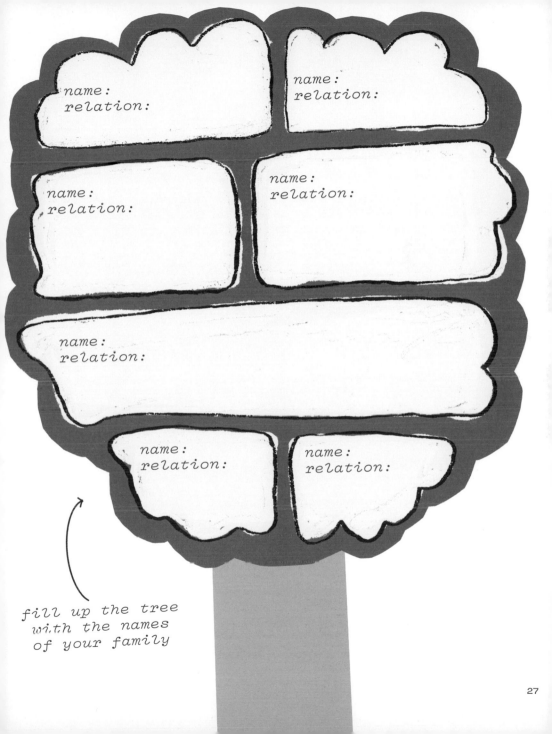

name:
relation:

name:
relation:

name:
relation:

name:
relation:

name:
relation:

name:
relation:

name:
relation:

fill up the tree with the names of your family

LOOK
at the size

of those paws!

your growth chart

~~~~~

date .... weight ....

date .... weight ....

date .... weight ....

date .... weight ....

date .... weight ....

date .... weight ....

date .... weight ....

date .... weight ....

date .... weight ....

date .... weight ....

date .... weight ....

date .... weight ....

date .... weight ....

date .... weight ....

YOUR

paw sinality

Your favorite dog treats...

....

....

....

And human treats...

....

....

....

Your favorite games...

....

....

....

....

Your reaction when we leave...

....

....

....

And come home...

....

....

....

Favorite cuddle position...

....

Your favorite nap spots...

....

....

....

Your favorite places for scratches...

....

....

How you act when you're home alone...

you're an angel ●————————————————● *you destroy everything*

Things you like to bark at...

....

....

....

....

Your best doggie friends...

....

....

how you feel about...

circle one

~~~~~~~

- 🙂 🙁 *swimming*
- 🙂 🙁 *bathing*
- 🙂 🙁 *fireworks*
- 🙂 🙁 *thunderstorms*
- 🙂 🙁 *snow*
- 🙂 🙁 *car rides*
- 🙂 🙁 *other dogs*

chewing chronicles

all of my attempts to train you

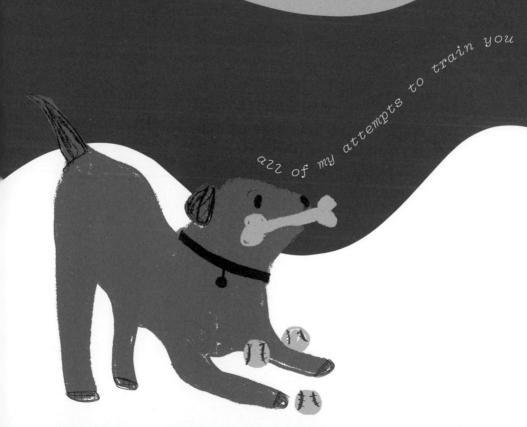

How you did in obedience classes (on a scale of 1–10)...

worst...   *best!*

①———②———③———④———⑤———⑥———⑦———⑧———⑨———⑩

1   2   3   4   5   6   7   8   9   10

Tricks you've learned...   **Things you'll never learn...**

....

....

....

....

....

How you like to beg...

....

....

....

....

How you behave at daycare or boarding...

....

....

....

....

Things you like to chew...

....

....

....

....

How long your toys last...

....

....

How you walk on a leash...

....

....

....

What you do when the doorbell rings...

....

....

....

What motivates you to learn a new trick...

....

....

....

how long before i let you...

~~~~~

♥ *get on the couch*

....

♥ *get on the bed*

....

♥ *eat from the dinner table*

....

♥ *off the leash*

....

♥ *start dictating my schedule*

....

♥ *become an excuse to not go somewhere*

....

barking

bad

your mischief

& mayhem

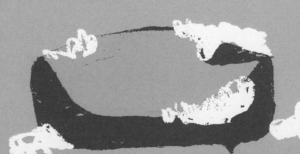

Your bad habits...

....

....

....

Things you've destroyed...

....

....

....

....

Things you've tried to eat...

....

....

....

Greatest escapes...

....

....

....

....

....

....

Favorite human foods...

....

....

....

....

People you love to bark at...

....

....

....

....

Furniture you love to sit on...

....

....

....

....

Favorite articles of clothing to steal...

....

....

....

....

Funniest "bad dog" moment...

....

....

....

....

....

....

....

How you try to get my attention...

....

....

....

Favorite things to hide from me...

....

....

....

Things I simply can't buy you...

.... | ....

.... | ....

.... | ....

 # mischief memories

date ....

mischief ....

....

....

....

....

date ....

mischief ....

....

....

....

....

date ....

mischief ....

....

....

....

....

mischief memories

date ....

mischief ....

....

....

....

....

date ....

mischief ....

....

....

....

....

date ....

mischief ....

....

....

....

the most
impressive
mischief

the most
impressive
mischief

tail WAGGERS

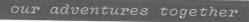

our adventures together

First road trip...

Date..

Where we went ....

....

First overnight trip...

Date..

Where we went ....

....

First night apart...

Date..

Where we went ....

....

Favorite walking/hiking paths...

....

....

....

Critters you like to chase...

....

....

....

Places we like to go together...

....

....

....

....

Where you like to sit in the car (check one)...

- *in someone's lap*
- *on the floor*
- *your car seat*
- *shotgun*

How often we need to stop on car rides to stretch your legs...

....

Favorite car music...

....

....

....

First airplane ride...

Date ....

Where we went ....

....

how you feel about...

circle one

~~~~~

🙂 🙁 *car windows down*

🙂 🙁 *long car rides*

🙂 🙁 *airplanes*

🙂 🙁 *airports*

🙂 🙁 *hiking*

🙂 🙁 *overnight trips*

🙂 🙁 *dog parks*

 let's keep adventuring

date ....

what went down ....

....

....

....

....

date ....

what went down ....

....

....

....

....

date ....

what went down ....

....

....

....

....

 let's keep adventuring

date ....

what went down ....

....

....

....

....

date ....

what went down ....

....

....

....

....

date ....

what went down ....

....

....

....

....

all of our
adventure pics

another
adventure pic

howli days

the life
of every party

your howloween costumes

～～～

year .... *costume* ....

year .... *costume* ....

year .... *costume* ....

year .... *costume* ....

year .... *costume* ....

year .... *costume* ....

year .... *costume* ....

year .... *costume* ....

year .... *costume* ....

year .... *costume* ....

your
first
howloween

us on
howloween

you and your friends →

your best costume ←

howliday celebrations

~~~

date .... *celebration* ....
gifts ....

date .... *celebration* ....
gifts ....

date .... *celebration* ....
gifts ....

date .... *celebration* ....
gifts ....

date .... *celebration* ....
gifts ....

date .... *celebration* ....
gifts ....

date .... *celebration* ....
gifts ....

date .... *celebration* ....
gifts ....

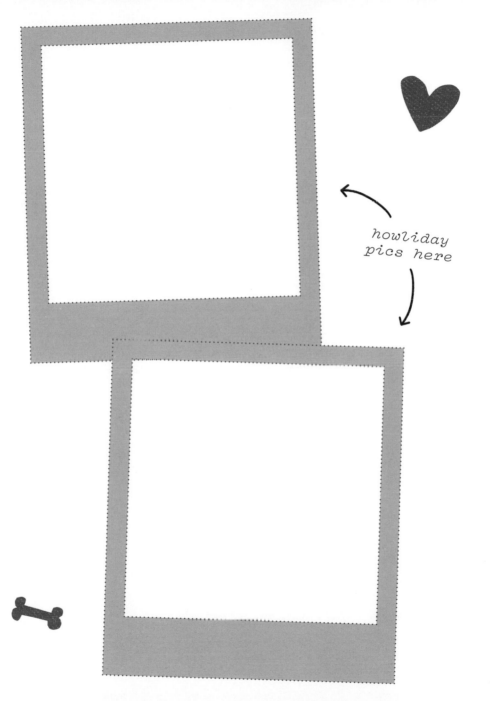

howliday pics here

birthday celebrations

~~~~~

date .... *location* ....
gifts ....
....

date .... *location* ....
gifts ....
....

date .... *location* ....
gifts ....
....

date .... *location* ....
gifts ....
....

date .... *location* ....
gifts ....
....

birthday celebrations

date .... location ....
gifts ....
....

date .... location ....
gifts ....
....

date .... location ....
gifts ....
....

date .... location ....
gifts ....
....

date .... location ....
gifts ....
....

birthday
pics here

more birthday
pics here

HOT dog

your greatest achievements

trick .... date ....

trick .... date ....

trick .... date ....

trick .... date ....

trick .... date ....

trick .... date ....

trick .... date ....

trick .... date ....

trick .... date ....

trick .... date ....

trick .... date ....

trick .... date ....

tricks in action

more
tricks in
action

quite
fetching

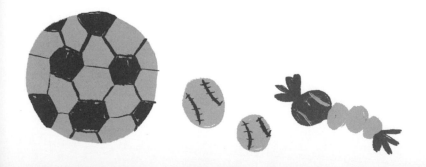

all the compliments you get

How you've changed my life...

*more
pup-a-razzi
photos here*

more memories

date ....

memory ....

....

....

....

....

....

....

....

....

date ....

memory ....

....

....

....

....

....

....

....

....

more memories

date ....

memory ....

....

....

....

....

....

....

....

....

date ....

memory ....

....

....

....

....

....

....

....

....

more memories

date ....

memory ....
....
....
....
....
....
....
....
....

date ....

memory ....
....
....
....
....
....
....
....
....

♥ more memories ♥

date ....

memory ....
....
....
....
....
....
....
....
....

date ....

memory ....
....
....
....
....
....
....
....

♥ more memories ♥

date ....

memory ....

....

....

....

....

....

....

....

date ....

memory ....

....

....

....

....

....

....

....

 more memories

date ....

memory ....

....

....

....

....

....

....

....

date ....

memory ....

....

....

....

....

....

....

....

more memories

date ....

memory ....

....

....

....

....

....

....

....

....

date ....

memory ....

....

....

....

....

....

....

....

....

more memories

date ....

memory ....

....

....

....

....

....

....

....

date ....

memory ....

....

....

....

....

....

....

....

 more memories

date ....

memory ....
....
....
....
....
....
....
....
....

date ....

memory ....
....
....
....
....
....
....
....
....

more memories

date ....

memory ....

....

....

....

....

....

....

....

date ....

memory ....

....

....

....

....

....

....

....

 more memories

date ....

memory ....
....
....
....
....
....
....
....
....

date ....

memory ....
....
....
....
....
....
....
....

more memories

date ....

memory ....

....

....

....

....

....

....

....

date ....

memory ....

....

....

....

....

....

....

....

 more memories

date ....

memory ....
....
....
....
....
....
....
....
....

date ....

memory ....
....
....
....
....
....
....
....

more memories

date ....

memory ....

....

....

....

....

....

....

....

....

date ....

memory ....

....

....

....

....

....

....

....

 more memories

date ....

memory ....

....

....

....

....

....

....

....

....

date ....

memory ....

....

....

....

....

....

....

....

....

The creation of this book would not have been possible without
the loving support (and slobber) of the Blue Star Press pups:

Published by Blue Star Press
PO Box 8835, Bend, OR 97708
contact@bluestarpress.com
www.bluestarpress.com

ISBN: 9781950968466

Printed in China

10 9 8 7 6 5 4 3 2 1